MORE

Love Talks

FOR COUPLES

101 Questions to Stimulate Interaction with Your Spouse

NORTHFIELD PUBLISHING
CHICAGO

Entry #28 first appeared in Ramon Presson, *Soul Care* (Littleton, Colo.: Serendipity House, 2000).

ISBN: 1-881273-50-4

1 3 5 7 9 10 8 6 4 2

Printed in the United States of America

Tips for Using More Love Talks

Your spouse is a fascinating person, a treasure trove of meaningful, humorous, and profound experiences, thoughts, feelings, ideas, memories, hopes, dreams, beliefs, and convictions. These questions celebrate the depth and wonderful mystery of your mate. Questions invite disclosure, and disclosure launches discovery. Discovery enriches a marriage and builds intimacy. Use the following 101 questions to prompt meaningful, in-depth discussions and to affirm and encourage your spouse.

Here are some ways to use the questions:

- During dinner at home (if you don't have children)
- During a quiet moment in the evening
- At bedtime (if both of you are alert)
- During dinner on a date night
- While in the car during a long drive

While the easiest way to proceed through the questions is to use them in the order they are presented, another possibility is that your spouse and you take turns in selecting the questions. We recommend that you do only one or two questions at a time. These questions are like dessert—a small and satisfying portion creates the anticipation for more later. *More Love Talks* offers a process to enjoy, not a project to complete.

Have fun with these questions two or three times each week and watch intimacy grow in your marriage.

What was something that you really wanted to do but were not allowed to do as a child or teen?

— QUESTION 1 —

What was something that you really wanted to do

but were not allowed to do as a child or teen?

What is one of the best/worst

customer service experiences you've had?

MORE
Love Talks
FOR COUPLES

*W*hat is one of the best/worst

customer service experiences you've had?

MORE
Love Talks
FOR COUPLES

— QUESTION 3 —

*What is one saying, quote, or Bible verse
that you strongly identify with?*

MORE
Love Talks
FOR COUPLES

— QUESTION 3 —

What is one saying, quote, or Bible verse that you strongly identify with?

MORE
Love Talks
FOR COUPLES

The airline overbooked our flight and we
voluntarily gave up our seats in exchange for
two round-trip tickets to any destination in
the United States, excluding Hawaii and Alaska.
Where do you want to go, and what time of year?

More
Love Talks
FOR COUPLES

The airline overbooked our flight and we voluntarily gave up our seats in exchange for two round-trip tickets to any destination in the United States, excluding Hawaii and Alaska. Where do you want to go, and what time of year?

— QUESTION 5 —

In Joshua 13:1 God tells Joshua that in spite of his advanced years there is still much land to be conquered. Do you have some "land" you still want to "conquer," something you want to accomplish?

In Joshua 13:1 God tells Joshua that in spite of his advanced years there is still much land to be conquered. Do you have some "land" you still want to "conquer," something you want to accomplish?

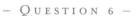

Recall something you experienced or a place you visited that didn't live up to the promotion or your expectations.

Recall something you experienced or a place you visited that didn't live up to the promotion or your expectations.

MORE
Love Talks
FOR COUPLES

— QUESTION 7 —

What is something humorous you recall about our first weeks or months of dating?

MORE
Love Talks
FOR COUPLES

*What is something humorous you recall about
our first weeks or months of dating?*

MORE
Love Talks
FOR COUPLES

What was one of the most inspiring

funerals or memorial services

you have ever attended?

MORE
Love Talks
FOR COUPLES

What was one of the most inspiring

funerals or memorial services

you have ever attended?

Complete the following: "I wish we could travel

to _____ and have _____

for breakfast/lunch/dinner/dessert."

*C*omplete the following: "I wish we could travel

to _____ and have _____

for breakfast/lunch/dinner/dessert."

What is something that was common
to you as a child—so common that you did
not keep it but you wish you had because it is
considered valuable today?

More
Love Talks
FOR COUPLES

What is something that was common to you as a child—so common that you did not keep it but you wish you had because it is considered valuable today?

— QUESTION 11 —

If you could own and operate your own business (and be guaranteed of its success), what would it be?

MORE
Love Talks
FOR COUPLES

If you could own and operate your own business (and be guaranteed of its success), what would it be?

MORE
Love Talks
FOR COUPLES

*If you had to give up sight, hearing,
the ability to speak, or the ability to walk,
which would you choose? Which would you be
most resistant to giving up?*

MORE
Love Talks
FOR COUPLES

*If you had to give up sight, hearing,
the ability to speak, or the ability to walk,
which would you choose? Which would you be
most resistant to giving up?*

If you could have four different homes
and live in four different parts of the U.S. during
the four seasons, state the location and season
that you would live in these homes.

*If you could have four different homes
and live in four different parts of the U.S. during
the four seasons, state the location and season
that you would live in these homes.*

MORE
Love Talks
FOR COUPLES

– QUESTION 14 –

*What famous person (living)
would you like to meet?*

MORE
Love Talks
FOR COUPLES

What famous person (living)
would you like to meet?

Name one or two books, other than the Bible,
that have significantly influenced your thinking.

Name one or two books, other than the Bible, that have significantly influenced your thinking.

MORE
Love Talks
FOR COUPLES

Usually "new" is presumed to also mean "improved." What is something you wish had not changed over the years?

More
Love Talks
FOR COUPLES

— QUESTION 16 —

Usually "new" is presumed to also mean "improved." What is something you wish had not changed over the years?

MORE
Love Talks
FOR COUPLES

If you had a magic wand and could change
anything in your life right now, what would you change?

If you had a magic wand and could change
anything in your life right now, what would you change?

*One of life's great delights is surprising
someone. Recall participating in a wonderful
surprise by doing one or more of the following:*

☐ *Presenting a special gift*

☐ *Plotting and/or attending a surprise party*

☐ *Your unexpected appearance or phone call*

*O*ne of life's great delights is surprising

someone. Recall participating in a wonderful

surprise by doing one or more of the following:

☐ *Presenting a special gift*

☐ *Plotting and/or attending a surprise party*

☐ *Your unexpected appearance or phone call*

— QUESTION 19 —

*If you could own a prop from a favorite movie
or television show, what would be the prop?*

(Some examples to spur your imagination: Dorothy's red shoes from The Wizard of Oz,

a light saber from Star Wars, Barney Fife's pistol, one of James Bond's cars,

a lab coat from ER, Moses' staff from The Ten Commandments,

the volleyball from Cast Away, a basketball from Hoosiers)

MORE
Love Talks
FOR COUPLES

— QUESTION 19 —

If you could own a prop from a favorite movie
or television show, what would be the prop?

(Some examples to spur your imagination: Dorothy's red shoes from The Wizard of Oz,

a light saber from Star Wars, Barney Fife's pistol, one of James Bond's cars,

a lab coat from ER, Moses' staff from The Ten Commandments,

the volleyball from Cast Away, a basketball from Hoosiers)

MORE
Love Talks
FOR COUPLES

If you could free someone of a burden,

who would that be?

If you could free someone of a burden,

who would that be?

MORE
Love Talks
FOR COUPLES

*What are two things that happened
today, and how did you feel about them?*

What are two things that happened
today, and how did you feel about them?

MORE
Love Talks
FOR COUPLES

— QUESTION 22 —

Name someone with whom you have lost contact
over the years and wonder how the person's doing.

MORE
Love Talks
FOR COUPLES

Name someone with whom you have lost contact
over the years and wonder how the person's doing.

— QUESTION 23 —

Name something in your hometown that has been torn down and/or replaced, and describe how you feel about it being gone.

— QUESTION 23 —

Name something in your hometown that has been torn down and/or replaced, and describe how you feel about it being gone.

MORE
Love Talks
FOR COUPLES

What were some of the surprises
at the last class reunion you attended?

What were some of the surprises
at the last class reunion you attended?

MORE
Love Talks
FOR COUPLES

What is one of the most difficult

transitions you have ever made?

What is one of the most difficult transitions you have ever made?

More
Love Talks
FOR COUPLES

— QUESTION 26 —

*If you knew that your very next prayer
would be answered, what would you ask God for?*

If you knew that your very next prayer would be answered, what would you ask God for?

MORE
Love Talks
FOR COUPLES

Name the person you know
who most personifies perseverance.

*Name the person you know
who most personifies perseverance.*

MORE
Love Talks
FOR COUPLES

While your partner is shopping across the street,
you have an hour to browse in a large bookstore. In what
two sections are you likely to spend most of your time?

☐ *Fiction* ☐ *Magazines* ☐ *Religious/inspirational* ☐ *Children's books* ☐ *Biography*

☐ *Marriage/parenting* ☐ *Arts & crafts* ☐ *Personal finance* ☐ *Psychology/self-help*

☐ *Literature* ☐ *Hobbies* ☐ *Career/management/ leadership*

☐ *Sports* ☐ *Humor* ☐ *Other_____*

More
Love Talks
FOR COUPLES

While your partner is shopping across the street, you have an hour to browse in a large bookstore. In what two sections are you likely to spend most of your time?

☐ Fiction ☐ Magazines ☐ Religious/inspirational ☐ Children's books ☐ Biography

☐ Marriage/parenting ☐ Arts & crafts ☐ Personal finance ☐ Psychology/self-help

☐ Literature ☐ Hobbies ☐ Career/management/ leadership

☐ Sports ☐ Humor ☐ Other_____

More
Love Talks
FOR COUPLES

*R*ecall a time when you felt the actions
of a person or group grossly misrepresented the
true character and person of Christ.

Recall a time when you felt the actions of a person or group grossly misrepresented the true character and person of Christ.

MORE
Love Talks
FOR COUPLES

*Recall a time when adversity
became a catalyst for spiritual growth.*

*Recall a time when adversity
became a catalyst for spiritual growth.*

MORE
Love Talks
FOR COUPLES

If you could have any entertainer perform

for your birthday, whom would you choose?

If you could have any entertainer perform for your birthday, whom would you choose?

MORE
Love Talks
FOR COUPLES

$\mathcal{W}$hich person in the Bible
do you most identify with?

MORE
Love Talks
FOR COUPLES

*Which person in the Bible
do you most identify with?*

What talent or skill do you wish you possessed?

What talent or skill do you wish you possessed?

MORE
Love Talks
FOR COUPLES

If you could demonstrate patience in one area of life, what would it be?

*If you could demonstrate patience
in one area of life, what would it be?*

MORE
Love Talks
FOR COUPLES

— QUESTION 35 —

Jesus asked Peter, James, and John to accompany Him into the Garden of Gethsemane. Which three people would you ask to join you in praying during a crisis?

MORE
Love Talks
FOR COUPLES

Jesus asked Peter, James, and John to accompany Him into the Garden of Gethsemane. Which three people would you ask to join you in praying during a crisis?

MORE
Love Talks
FOR COUPLES

Name a well-known person that you've met.
How did you feel in his or her presence?

— QUESTION 36 —

Name a well-known person that you've met.
How did you feel in his or her presence?

MORE
Love Talks
FOR COUPLES

*Recall a favorite feature
about the home you grew up in. Recall a favorite
feature of the neighborhood.*

*Recall a favorite feature
about the home you grew up in. Recall a favorite
feature of the neighborhood.*

*What is something you would
not change about your life right now?*

MORE
Love Talks
FOR COUPLES

— QUESTION 38 —

What is something you would not change about your life right now?

MORE
Love Talks
FOR COUPLES

A project that I'm putting off is . . .

A project that I'm putting off is . . .

If your house was on fire and everyone
(including pets) was safe outside, and you could
safely retrieve one personal item (other than photo
albums), what would you choose?

MORE
Love Talks
FOR COUPLES

If your house was on fire and everyone (including pets) was safe outside, and you could safely retrieve one personal item (other than photo albums), what would you choose?

— QUESTION 41 —

If you were imprisoned for your faith
and could only have one book of the Bible with
you to read, what would you choose?

MORE
Love Talks
FOR COUPLES

*If you were imprisoned for your faith
and could only have one book of the Bible with
you to read, what would you choose?*

If you could adopt one personality trait from someone that you know, what would you take and from whom?

If you could adopt one personality trait from someone that you know, what would you take and from whom?

MORE
Love Talks
FOR COUPLES

Congratulations! You have the winning bid in an auction for items once owned by famous people (living or deceased). Name the famous original item and the item for which you bid.

Congratulations! You have the winning bid in an auction for items once owned by famous people (living or deceased). Name the famous original item and the item for which you bid.

MORE
Love Talks
FOR COUPLES

*If you could have been the creator
of any single piece of well-known art, music, or
literature, which would you choose?*

More
Love Talks
FOR COUPLES

If you could have been the creator of any single piece of well-known art, music, or literature, which would you choose?

MORE
Love Talks
FOR COUPLES

What is one of the most significant sermons, messages, or presentations you've ever heard? How did it impact you?

What is one of the most significant sermons, messages, or presentations you've ever heard? How did it impact you?

Imagine that you discover you're related to someone famous. Who would you like it to be, knowing that the discovery would mean a new and ongoing relationship?

— QUESTION 46 —

Imagine that you discover you're related to someone famous. Who would you like it to be, knowing that the discovery would mean a new and ongoing relationship?

MORE
Love Talks
FOR COUPLES

If you could find something in your attic that you thought was lost forever, what would it be?

MORE
Love Talks
FOR COUPLES

If you could find something in your attic

that you thought was lost forever, what would it be?

With whom among your deceased relatives do you wish you could have been better acquainted?

With whom among your deceased relatives do you wish you could have been better acquainted?

Recall one of the best days of your life,

when you felt especially alive and joyful.

MORE
Love Talks
FOR COUPLES

*Recall one of the best days of your life,
when you felt especially alive and joyful.*

MORE
Love Talks
FOR COUPLES

— QUESTION 50 —

Who is the best boss you've ever had?

MORE
Love Talks
FOR COUPLES

— QUESTION 50 —

Who is the best boss you've ever had?

MORE
Love Talks
FOR COUPLES

If you were suddenly gifted as a writer,
describe the first book you'd publish.

MORE
Love Talks
FOR COUPLES

*If you were suddenly gifted as a writer,
describe the first book you'd publish.*

MORE
Love Talks
FOR COUPLES

– QUESTION 52 –

Other than news of a death, what is the

most disturbing personal news you've ever received?

MORE
Love Talks
FOR COUPLES

Other than news of a death, what is the

most disturbing personal news you've ever received?

*Recall a time when you were
delighted or surprised to be chosen.*

Recall a time when you were delighted or surprised to be chosen.

MORE
Love Talks
FOR COUPLES

How would you feel if you were to learn that you were moving to another city in a few months? What would you miss the least? What and whom would you miss the most?

MORE
Love Talks
FOR COUPLES

How would you feel if you were to learn that you were moving to another city in a few months? What would you miss the least? What and whom would you miss the most?

MORE
Love Talks
FOR COUPLES

A "mulligan" is the second chance to hit
a golf shot after flubbing the first shot. Complete
this sentence: "Something in my life for which I
wished I could have played a mulligan is..."

MORE
Love Talks
FOR COUPLES

A "mulligan" is the second chance to hit
a golf shot after flubbing the first shot. Complete
this sentence: "Something in my life for which I
wished I could have played a mulligan is..."

If you could be on the cover
of any magazine, which one would it be, and what
would be the caption or headline?

MORE
Love Talks
FOR COUPLES

— QUESTION 56 —

*If you could be on the cover
of any magazine, which one would it be, and what
would be the caption or headline?*

MORE
Love Talks
FOR COUPLES

*Charlie Brown never successfully
kicked the football while Lucy was holding it for
him. How about your "almosts"? Complete this
sentence: "Sometimes I wonder if I will ever..."*

Charlie Brown never successfully kicked the football while Lucy was holding it for him. How about your "almosts"? Complete this sentence: "Sometimes I wonder if I will ever..."

MORE
Love Talks
FOR COUPLES

For what sports event would you

like to go back and reverse the outcome?

MORE
Love Talks
FOR COUPLES

For what sports event would you like to go back and reverse the outcome?

MORE
Love Talks
FOR COUPLES

*If you had access to any living
person for advice, whom would you call
and concerning what?*

MORE
Love Talks
FOR COUPLES

— QUESTION 59 —

If you had access to any living person for advice, whom would you call and concerning what?

*For what special location (or occasion)
would you like to have a special VIP pass?
For example: the White House or Carnegie Hall
(or the Olympics or Rose Bowl Parade)*

MORE
Love Talks
FOR COUPLES

*For what special location (or occasion)
would you like to have a special VIP pass?
For example: the White House or Carnegie Hall
(or the Olympics or Rose Bowl Parade)*

MORE
Love Talks
FOR COUPLES

— QUESTION 61 —

What is the hardest phone call

you've ever had to make?

What is the hardest phone call

you've ever had to make?

Of the people you know, who seems

most satisfied with his or her job?

What would be your dream job?

More

Love Talks

FOR COUPLES

Of the people you know, who seems

most satisfied with his or her job?

What would be your dream job?

MORE
Love Talks
FOR COUPLES

What do you think

is the toughest decision you ever made?

*W*hat do you think

is the toughest decision you ever made?

MORE
*L*ove *T*alks
FOR COUPLES

If you could give a substantial amount of money to someone in need right now, to whom would you give it?

MORE
Love Talks
FOR COUPLES

*If you could give a substantial amount
of money to someone in need right now,
to whom would you give it?*

– QUESTION 65 –

What is your favorite month of the year?

MORE
Love Talks
FOR COUPLES

What is your favorite month of the year?

*If you were a contestant on **Jeopardy,** what would you hope would be one of the categories?*

If you were a contestant on Jeopardy, *what would*

you hope would be one of the categories?

What do you think would be the hardest thing about being President of the United States? What aspect of the job do you think you would enjoy the most?

*W*hat do you think would be

the hardest thing about being President of the United States?

What aspect of the job do you think you would enjoy the most?

*Jacob tricked his brother, Esau,
and deceived his father, Isaac. Describe a time
when you were tricked or lied to.*

MORE
Love Talks
FOR COUPLES

Jacob tricked his brother, Esau, and deceived his father, Isaac. Describe a time when you were tricked or lied to.

MORE
Love Talks
FOR COUPLES

Recall a schoolboy/schoolgirl crush.

MORE
Love Talks
FOR COUPLES

Recall a schoolboy/schoolgirl crush.

*What birthday or holiday would
you like (or not like) to live over again?*

More
Love Talks
FOR COUPLES

*What birthday or holiday would
you like (or not like) to live over again?*

Describe a time when you lost

or broke something belonging to someone else.

Describe a time when you lost

or broke something belonging to someone else.

MORE
Love Talks
FOR COUPLES

*R*ecall an encounter with a snake,
mouse, spider, bee, toad, or any other creature
that gives you the creeps.

MORE
Love Talks
FOR COUPLES

*Recall an encounter with a snake,
mouse, spider, bee, toad, or any other creature
that gives you the creeps.*

More
Love Talks
FOR COUPLES

$\mathcal{M}y$ *first time on a stage that*

I can remember was . . .

My first time on a stage that

I can remember was . . .

Can you recall a time when you struggled

with doubt concerning one or more of the following:

☐ *God's existence*   ☐ *God's plan*

☐ *God's love*   ☐ *God's timing*

☐ *God's power*   ☐ *God's faithfulness*

☐ *God's justice*   ☐ *God's will*

☐ *God's wisdom*

Can you recall a time when you struggled

with doubt concerning one or more of the following:

☐ *God's existence* ☐ *God's plan*

☐ *God's love* ☐ *God's timing*

☐ *God's power* ☐ *God's faithfulness*

☐ *God's justice* ☐ *God's will*

☐ *God's wisdom*

What would you like to have season tickets to?

MORE
Love Talks
FOR COUPLES

What would you like to have season tickets to?

One of my disappointments from last year was . . .

MORE
Love Talks
FOR COUPLES

*O*ne of my disappointments from last year was . . .

If you could discover a cure for
any disease, what would it be?
(If you choose cancer, try to be specific.)

If you could discover a cure for
any disease, what would it be?
(If you choose cancer, try to be specific.)

MORE
Love Talks
FOR COUPLES

*R*ecall a movie whose ending you would like to
rewrite. How would your version end?

Recall a movie whose ending you would like to rewrite. How would your version end?

MORE
Love Talks
FOR COUPLES

If you could be fluent in another language,

which would you choose and why?

MORE
Love Talks
FOR COUPLES

If you could be fluent in another language,

which would you choose and why?

MORE
Love Talks
FOR COUPLES

*R*ecall a practical joke played on you
and/or recall one you played on someone else.

*R*ecall a practical joke played on you
and/or recall one you played on someone else.

MORE
Love Talks
FOR COUPLES

Create a new national holiday

commemorating an historical event or person.

What, why, and when?

MORE
Love Talks
FOR COUPLES

Create a new national holiday

commemorating an historical event or person.

What, why, and when?

David was tormented by an ungodly King Saul. Recall someone who had authority over you whom you found very difficult to respect.

David was tormented by an ungodly King Saul.
Recall someone who had authority over you whom
you found very difficult to respect.

MORE
Love Talks
FOR COUPLES

— QUESTION 83 —

*If you could have the speaking voice
of anyone you've heard, who would it be?
If you could have the singing voice of anyone
you've heard, who would it be?*

*If you could have the speaking voice
of anyone you've heard, who would it be?
If you could have the singing voice of anyone
you've heard, who would it be?*

MORE
Love Talks
FOR COUPLES

Each of you flip a coin

and answer the appropriate question below:

HEADS : *What was something encouraging*

or positive that happened today?

TAILS : *What was something disappointing*

or difficult that happened today?

*E*ach of you flip a coin

and answer the appropriate question below:

HEADS : *What was something encouraging*

or positive that happened today?

TAILS : *What was something disappointing*

or difficult that happened today?

MORE
Love Talks
FOR COUPLES

The Good Shepherd provides for, protects, and guides His sheep. Which of those three duties of the Shepherd is most meaningful and encouraging to you in your life right now?

The Good Shepherd provides for, protects, and guides His sheep. Which of those three duties of the Shepherd is most meaningful and encouraging to you in your life right now?

*Barnabas was an encourager and
mentor to the apostle Paul in the years
immediately following Paul's conversion.
Recall someone who was a spiritual encourager
or mentor to you for a season.*

*B*arnabas was an encourager and
mentor to the apostle Paul in the years
immediately following Paul's conversion.
Recall someone who was a spiritual encourager
or mentor to you for a season.

MORE
Love Talks
FOR COUPLES

Which of the Seven Natural Wonders of the World would you most like to see? Why this one wonder?

☐ *The Grand Canyon (Arizona)* ☐ *The Great Barrier Reef (Australia)*

☐ *Harbor of Rio de Janeiro (Brazil)* ☐ *The northern lights, or aurora borealis (Alaska);*

☐ *Mount Everest (Nepal/Tibet);* ☐ *Paricutin volcano (Mexico);*

☐ *Victoria Falls (Zimbabwe/Zambia)*

MORE
Love Talks
FOR COUPLES

Which of the Seven Natural Wonders of the World would you most like to see? Why this one wonder?

☐ *The Grand Canyon (Arizona)* ☐ *The Great Barrier Reef (Australia)*

☐ *Harbor of Rio de Janeiro (Brazil)* ☐ *The northern lights, or aurora borealis (Alaska);*

☐ *Mount Everest (Nepal/Tibet);* ☐ *Paricutin volcano (Mexico);*

☐ *Victoria Falls (Zimbabwe/Zambia)*

MORE
Love Talks
FOR COUPLES

If I were young again, I'd spend more time...

— QUESTION 88 —

If I were young again, I'd spend more time...

MORE
Love Talks
FOR COUPLES

*S*omething I miss is. . .

Something I miss is...

MORE
Love Talks
FOR COUPLES

If I had one year to live, something I'd like to do is . . .

MORE
Love Talks
FOR COUPLES

If I had one year to live, something I'd like to do is . . .

MORE
Love Talks
FOR COUPLES

*Peter said to Jesus, "We've fished all night
and haven't caught anything."
Is there any area of your life where you feel that
hard work is not paying off?*

MORE
Love Talks
FOR COUPLES

*Peter said to Jesus, "We've fished all night
and haven't caught anything."
Is there any area of your life where you feel that
hard work is not paying off?*

MORE
Love Talks
FOR COUPLES

*Jesus' disciples were rowing
the boat for several hours against a contrary wind.
Frustration is defined as a response
to a blocked goal. Is there any area where you feel
a goal or plan is being blocked?*

*Jesus' disciples were rowing
the boat for several hours against a contrary wind.
Frustration is defined as a response
to a blocked goal. Is there any area where you feel
a goal or plan is being blocked?*

More
Love Talks
FOR COUPLES

Peter was awestruck by his experience of seeing Moses, Elijah, and Jesus on the Mount of Transfiguration. Can you recall a spiritual experience that was so real and powerful that you did not want it to end?

MORE
Love Talks
FOR COUPLES

*Peter was awestruck by his experience
of seeing Moses, Elijah, and Jesus on the Mount
of Transfiguration. Can you recall a spiritual
experience that was so real and powerful that you
did not want it to end?*

MORE
Love Talks
FOR COUPLES

*I*magine that your internal dashboard has

a joy gauge on it. What is your present reading?

E _____

1/4 _____

1/2 _____

3/4 _____

F _____

MORE
Love Talks
FOR COUPLES

*Imagine that your internal dashboard has
a joy gauge on it. What is your present reading?*

E ____

¼ ____

½ ____

¾ ____

F ____

MORE
Love Talks
FOR COUPLES

Something about you

that I hope never changes is . . .

MORE
Love Talks
FOR COUPLES

Something about you

that I hope never changes is . . .

MORE
Love Talks
FOR COUPLES

*F*inish this sentence:

"I wish we'd had the camera with us when . . ."

MORE
Love Talks
FOR COUPLES

*F*inish this sentence:

"I wish we'd had the camera with us when . . ."

I think it would be wonderful to have

a hotel room in _____ and wake up the

first morning and throw open

the curtains to behold a magnificent view of

_____.

— QUESTION 97 —

I think it would be wonderful to have

a hotel room in _____ and wake up the

first morning and throw open

the curtains to behold a magnificent view of

_____.

MORE
Love Talks
FOR COUPLES

If you were to brag about me to your friends,

what would you tell them?

MORE

Love Talks

FOR COUPLES

– QUESTION 98 –

If you were to brag about me to your friends,

what would you tell them?

More
Love Talks
FOR COUPLES

You are the new owners of a six-bedroom
bed-and-breakfast inn. Where is it located? What will be
unique about it? What will you name it? Instead of numbering the
rooms, innkeepers frequently give each room a name based
on a theme. What will be your room theme? What will be
the name of your favorite room?

MORE
Love Talks
FOR COUPLES

You are the new owners of a six-bedroom bed-and-breakfast inn. Where is it located? What will be unique about it? What will you name it? Instead of numbering the rooms, innkeepers frequently give each room a name based on a theme. What will be your room theme? What will be the name of your favorite room?

Complete this sentence:

"It's too bad that kids today will never

know what it's like to . . ."

MORE
Love Talks
FOR COUPLES

Complete this sentence:
"It's too bad that kids today will never
know what it's like to . . ."

MORE
Love Talks
FOR COUPLES

— QUESTION 101 —

*Take a few minutes to review the first
one hundred items before answering this final one:
From our sharing responses to these questions and
statements, can you recall one of my answers that
especially interested or surprised you?*

More
Love Talks
FOR COUPLES

*T*ake a few minutes to review the first
one hundred items before answering this final one:
From our sharing responses to these questions and
statements, can you recall one of my answers that
especially interested or surprised you?